Caterpillars.

What will I be when I get to be me?

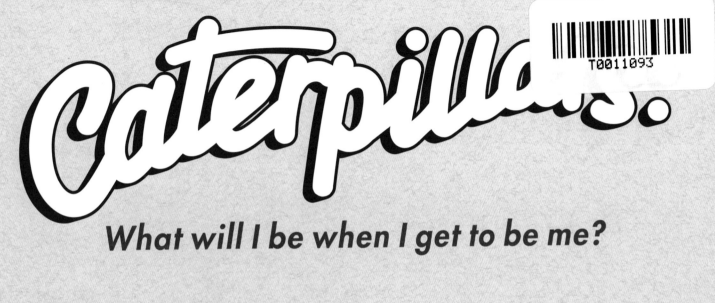

BURP!

A TOON BOOK BY
Kevin McCloskey

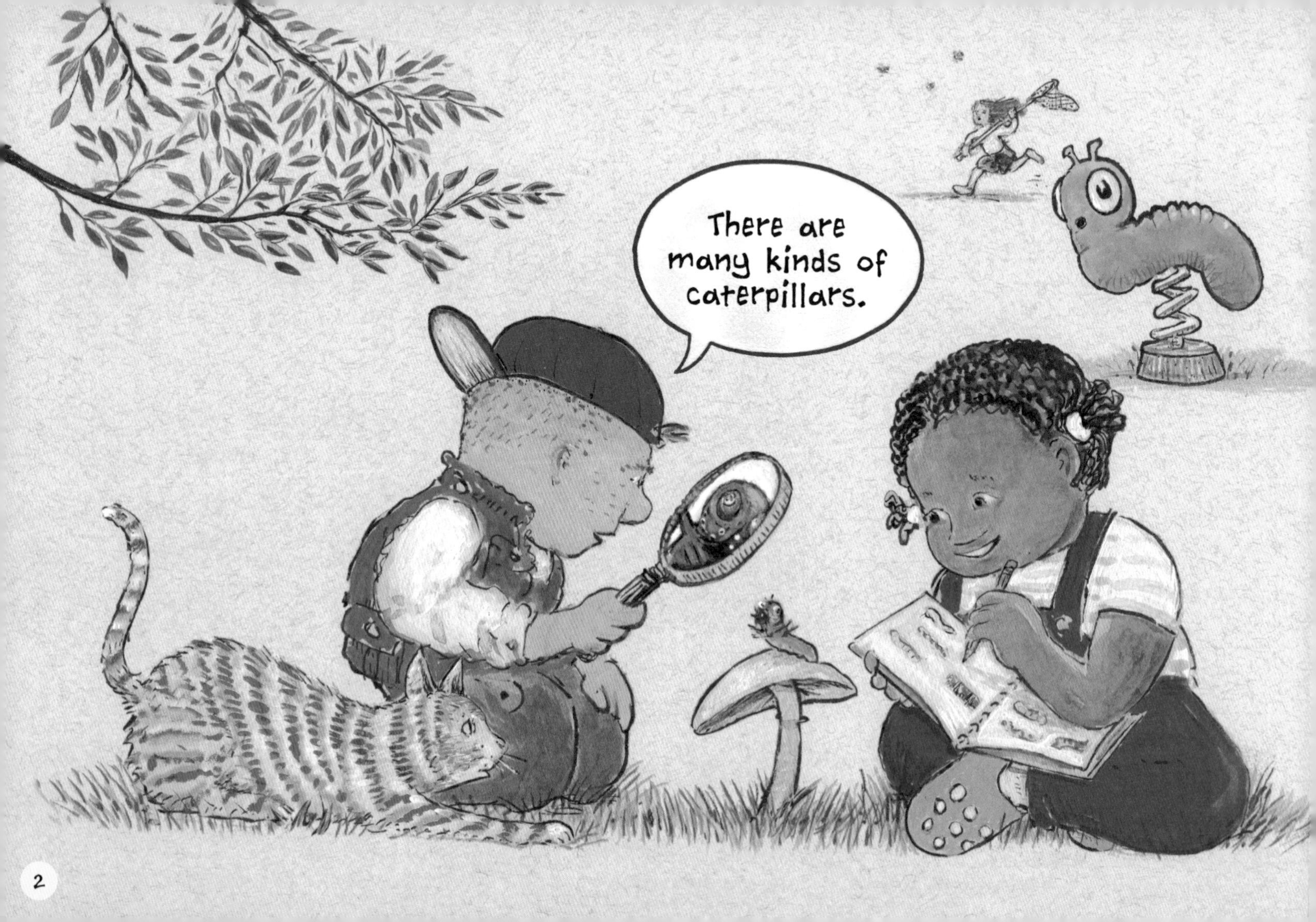
There are many kinds of caterpillars.

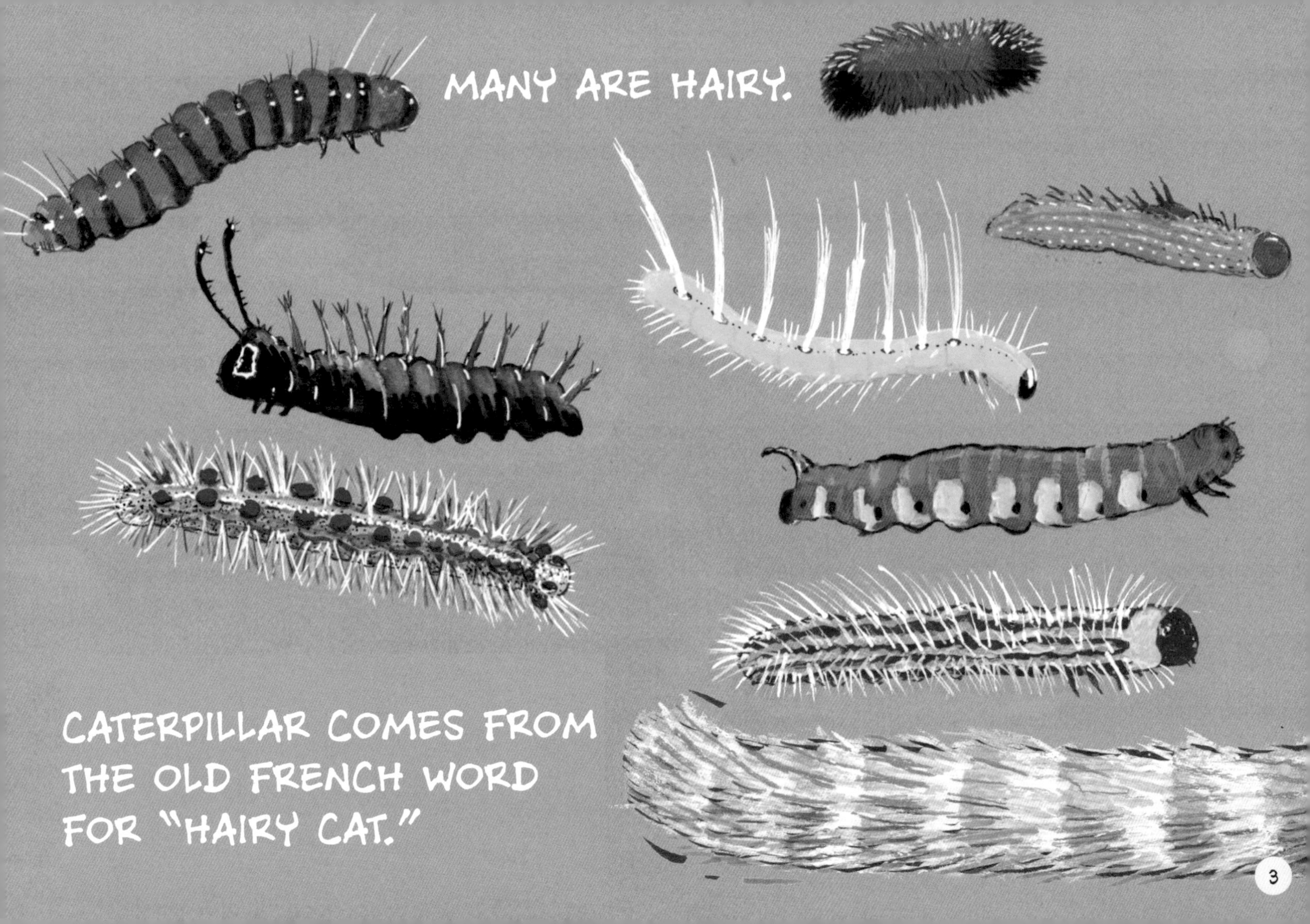

MANY ARE HAIRY.

CATERPILLAR COMES FROM THE OLD FRENCH WORD FOR "HAIRY CAT."

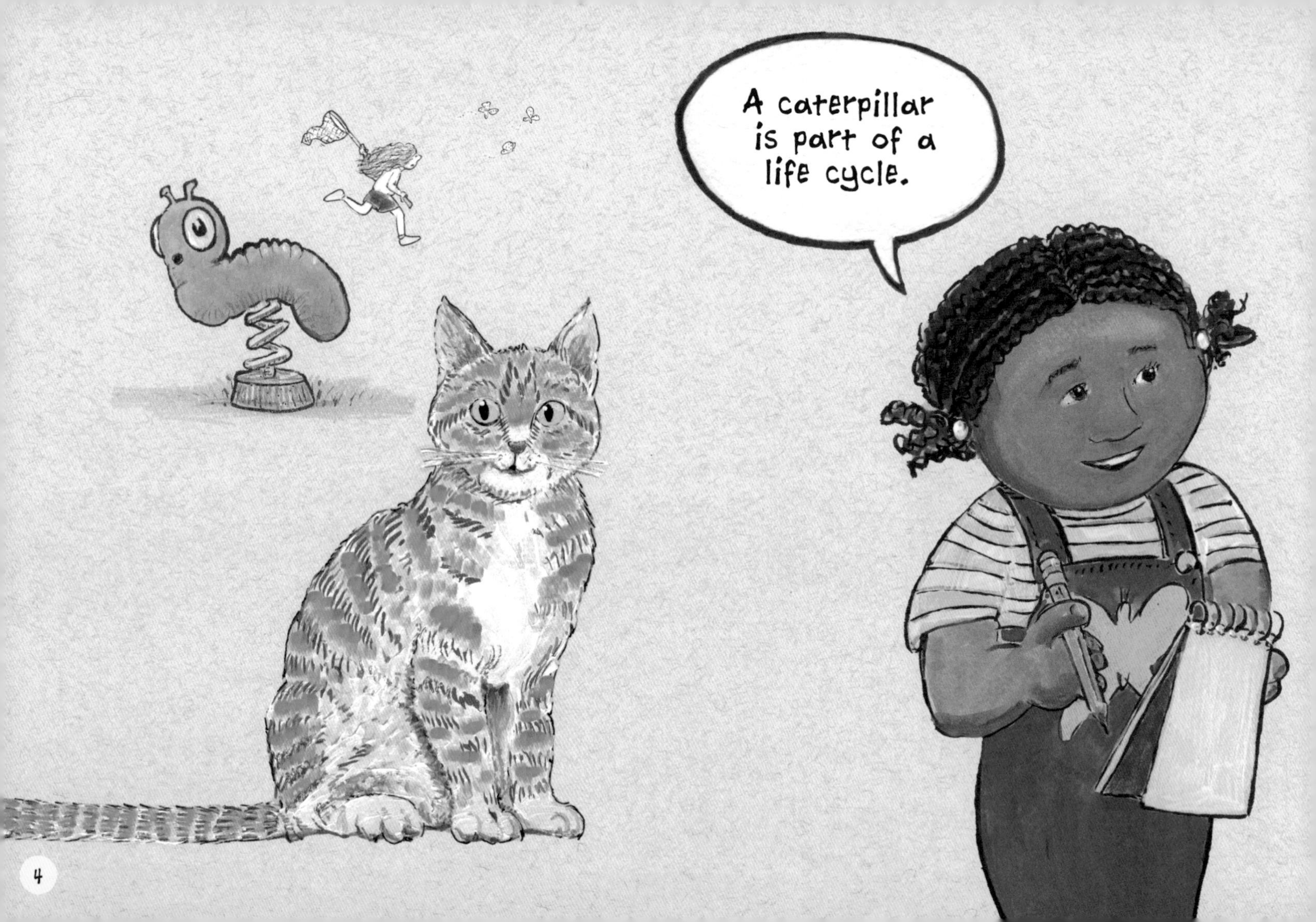
A caterpillar is part of a life cycle.

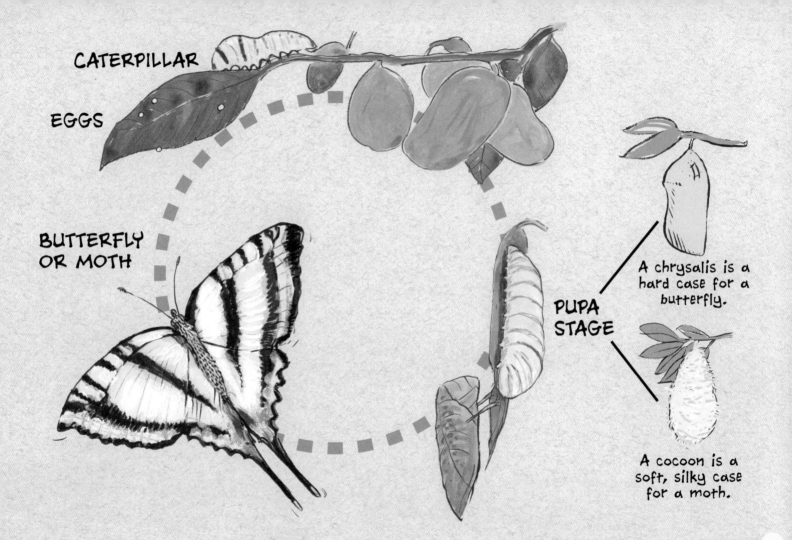

CATERPILLAR

EGGS

BUTTERFLY
OR MOTH

PUPA
STAGE

A chrysalis is a
hard case for a
butterfly.

A cocoon is a
soft, silky case
for a moth.

THE STORY STARTS WITH EGGS ON LEAVES.

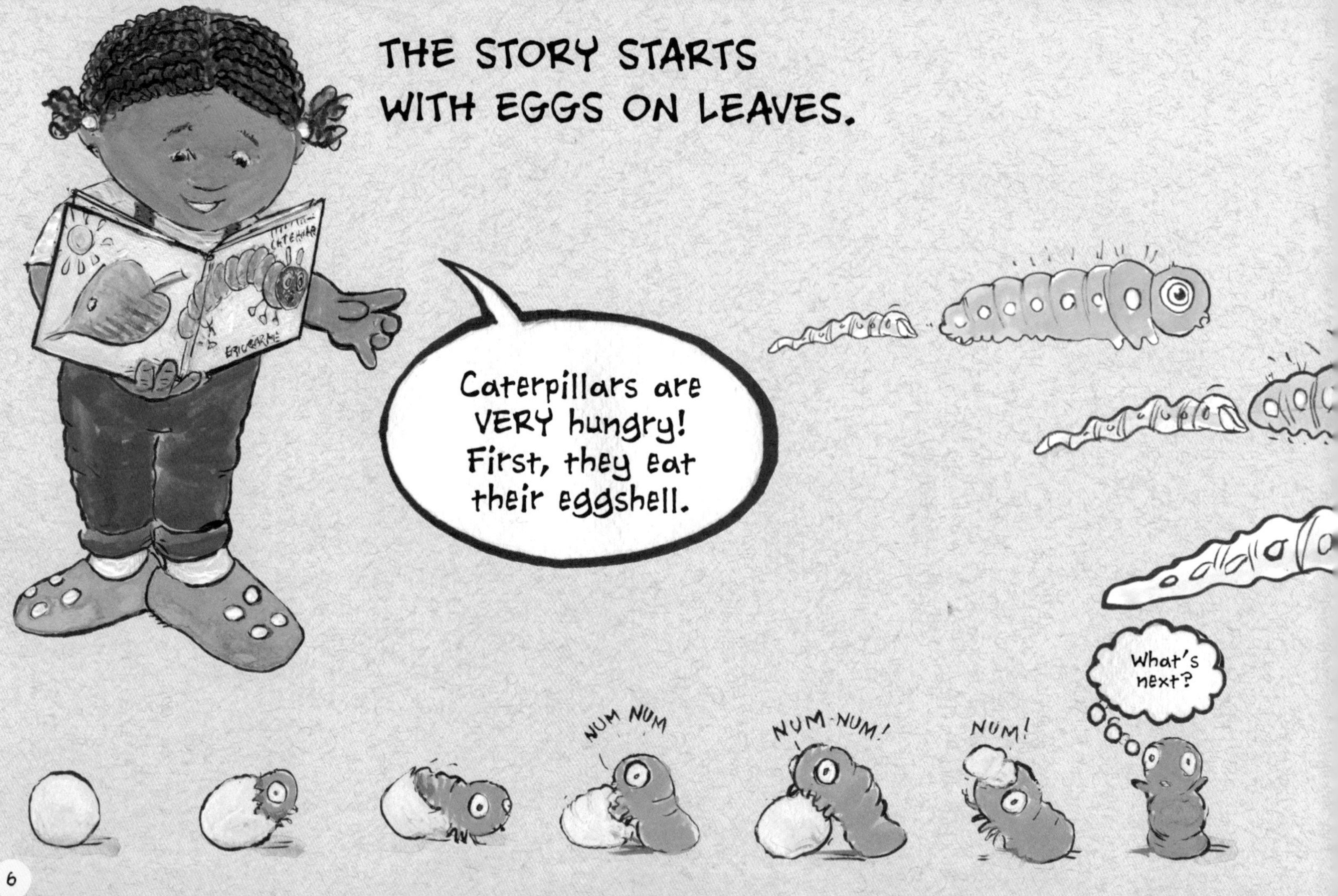

Caterpillars are VERY hungry! First, they eat their eggshell.
NUM NUM
NUM-NUM!
NUM!
What's next?

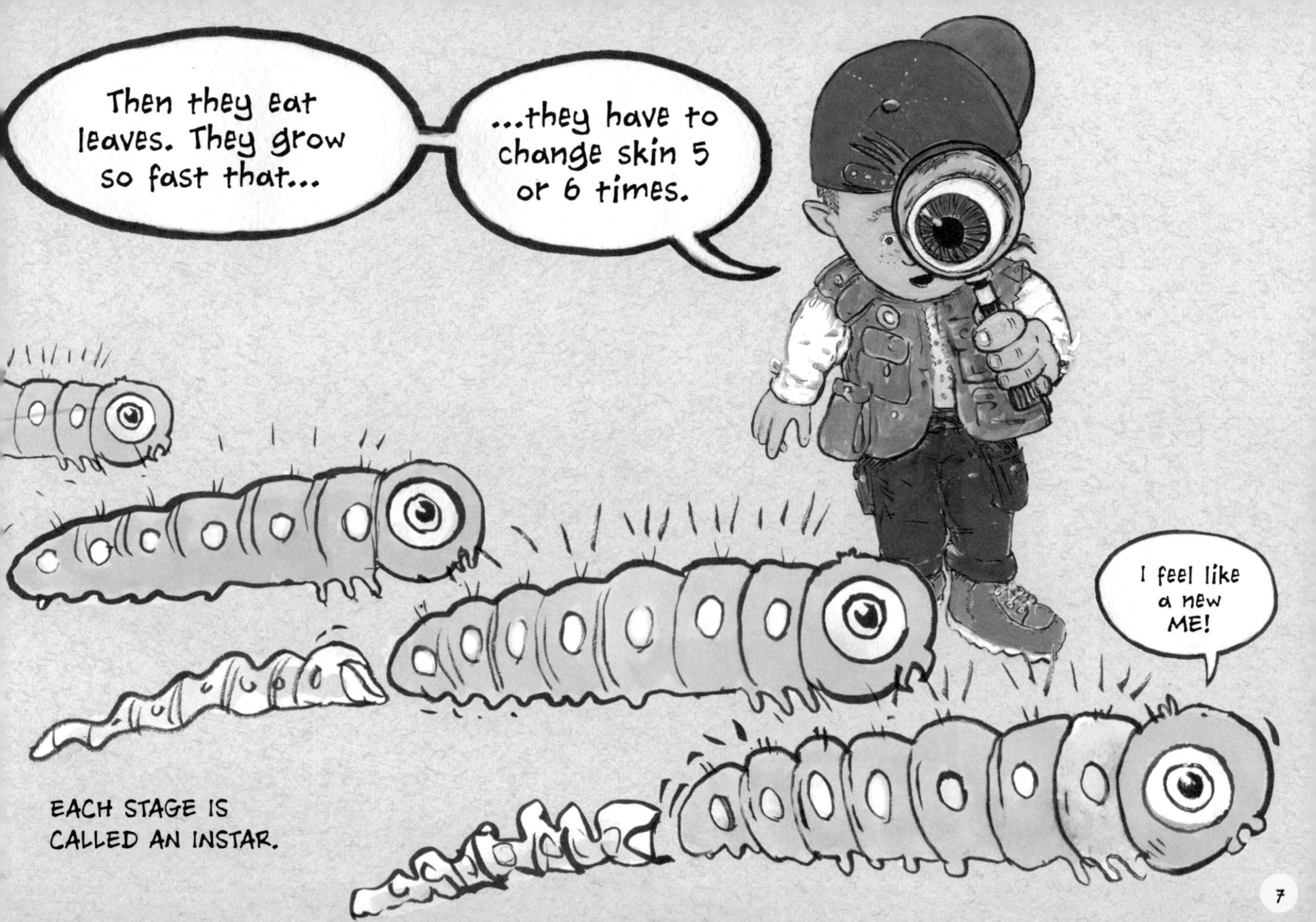
Then they eat leaves. They grow so fast that...
...they have to change skin 5 or 6 times.
I feel like a new ME!
EACH STAGE IS CALLED AN INSTAR.

A CATERPILLAR IS A TUBE WITH A STOMACH.

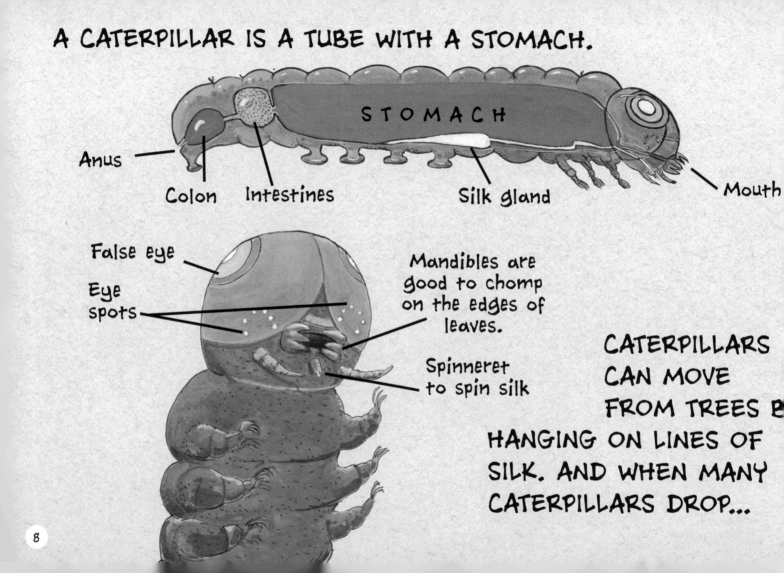

STOMACH

Anus

Colon   Intestines

Silk gland

Mouth

False eye

Eye spots

Mandibles are good to chomp on the edges of leaves.

Spinneret to spin silk

CATERPILLARS CAN MOVE FROM TREES B HANGING ON LINES OF SILK. AND WHEN MANY CATERPILLARS DROP...

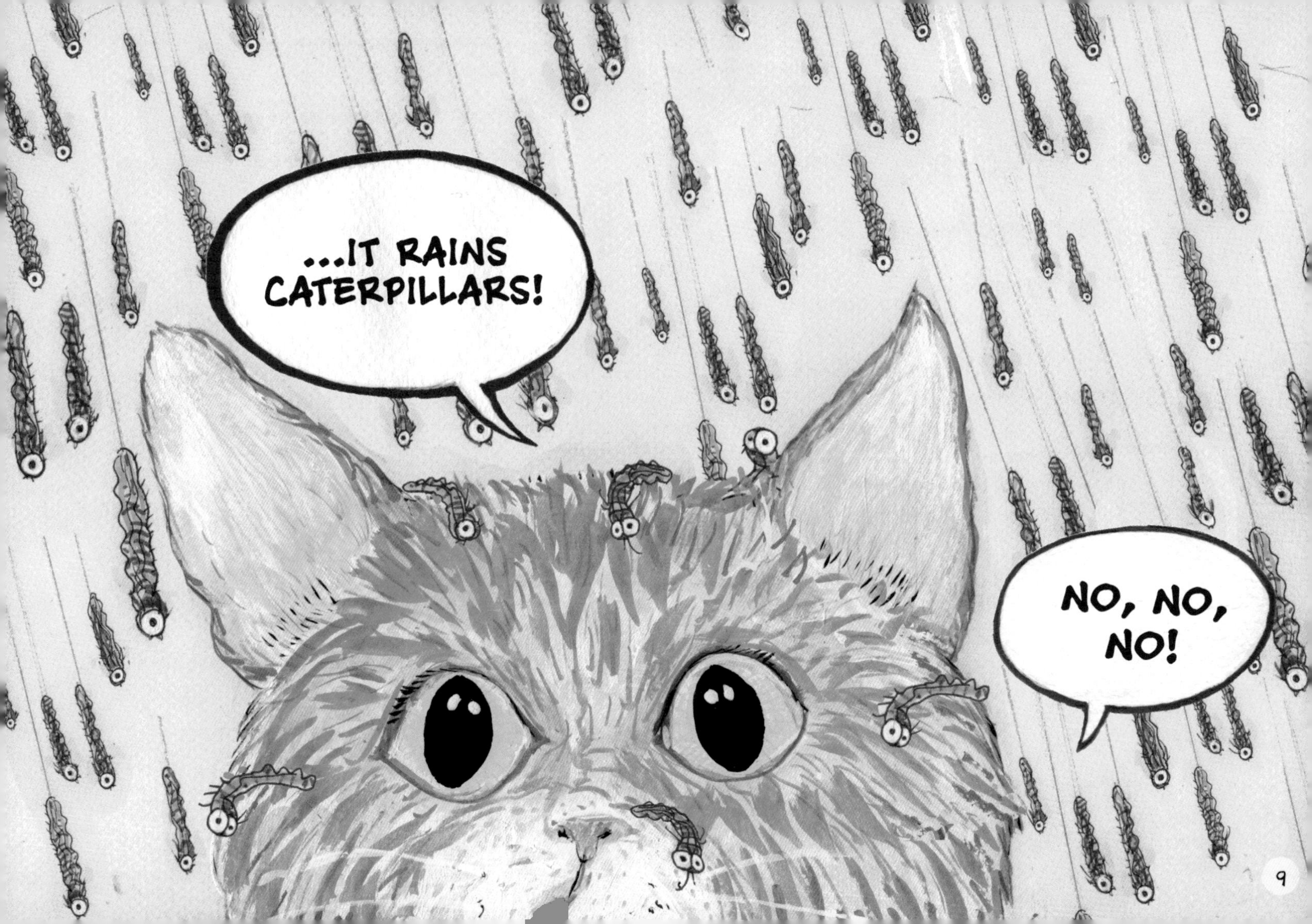
...IT RAINS CATERPILLARS!
NO, NO, NO!

THE SILKWORM CATERPILLAR FEEDS ON MULBERRY TREES.

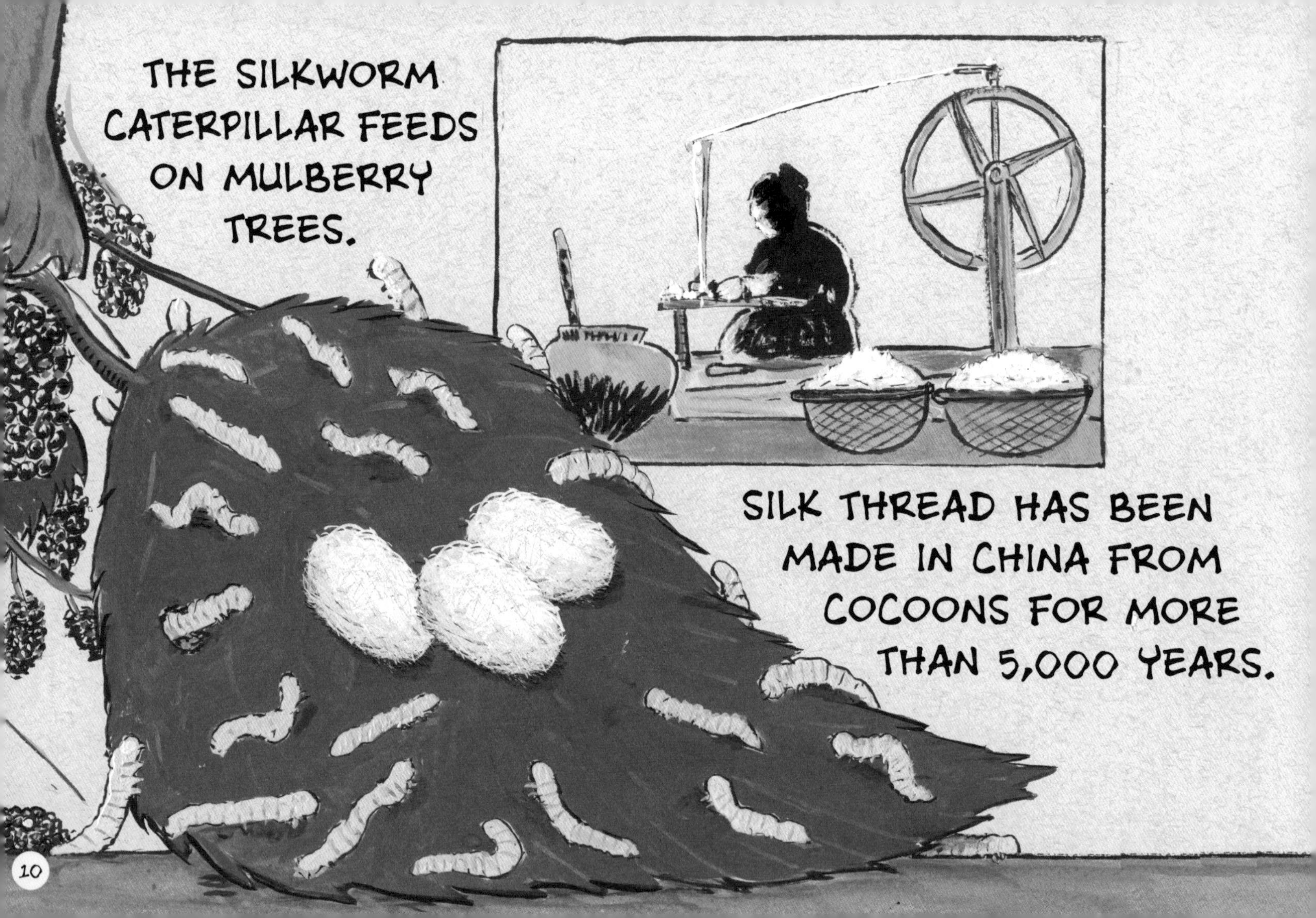

SILK THREAD HAS BEEN MADE IN CHINA FROM COCOONS FOR MORE THAN 5,000 YEARS.

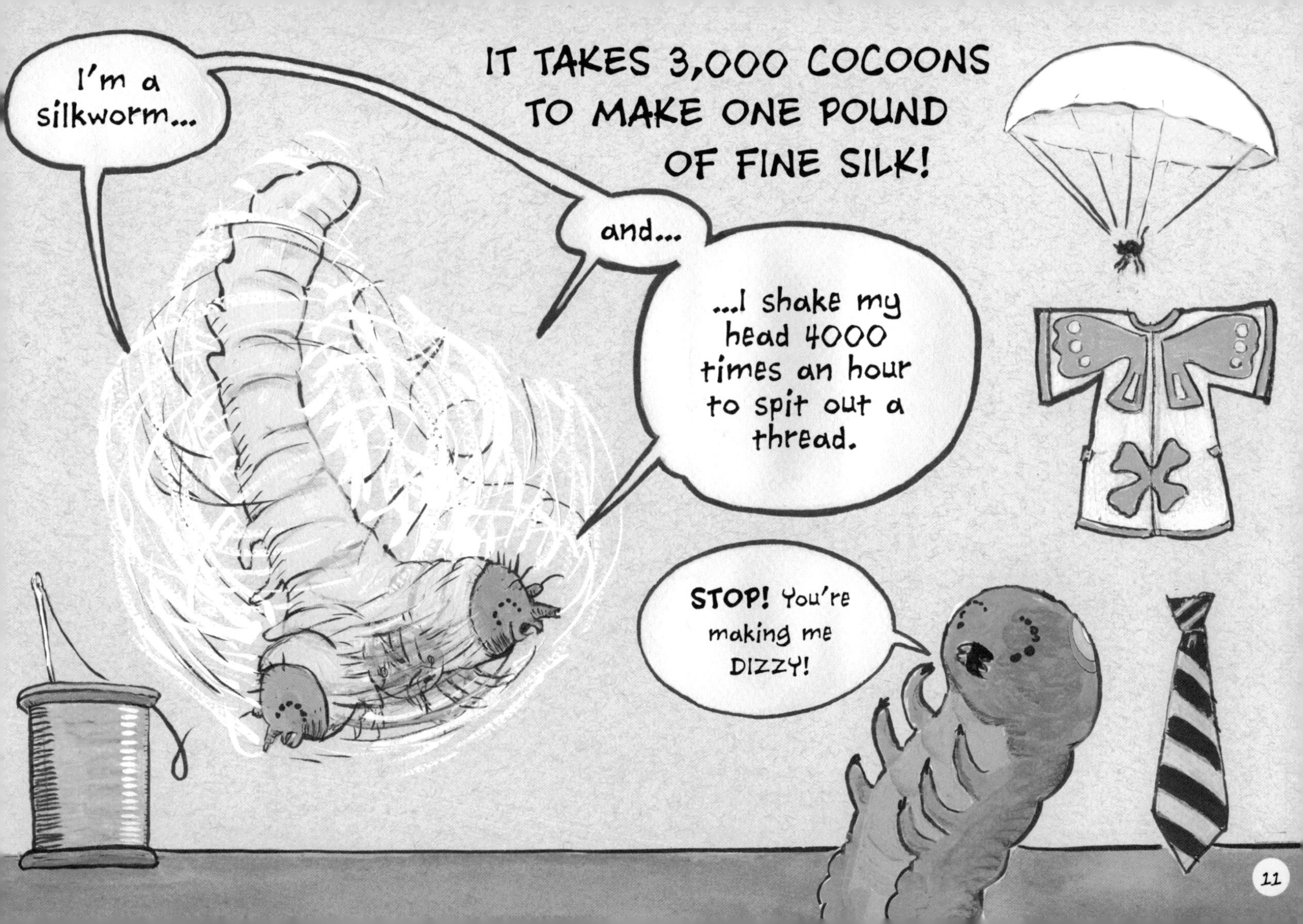
I'm a silkworm...
IT TAKES 3,000 COCOONS TO MAKE ONE POUND OF FINE SILK!
and...
...I shake my head 4000 times an hour to spit out a thread.
STOP! You're making me DIZZY!

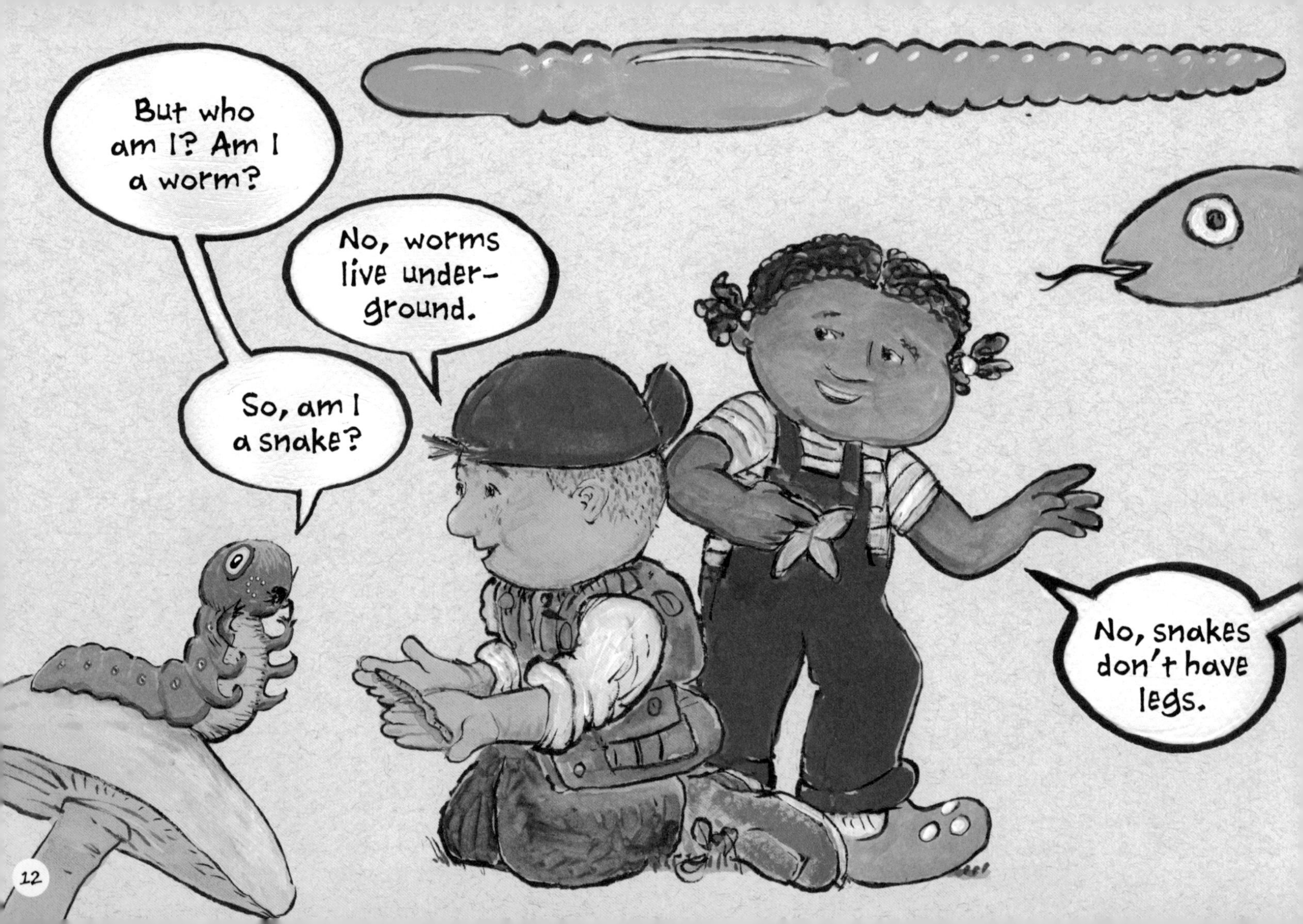
But who am I? Am I a worm?
No, worms live under-ground.
So, am I a snake?
No, snakes don't have legs.

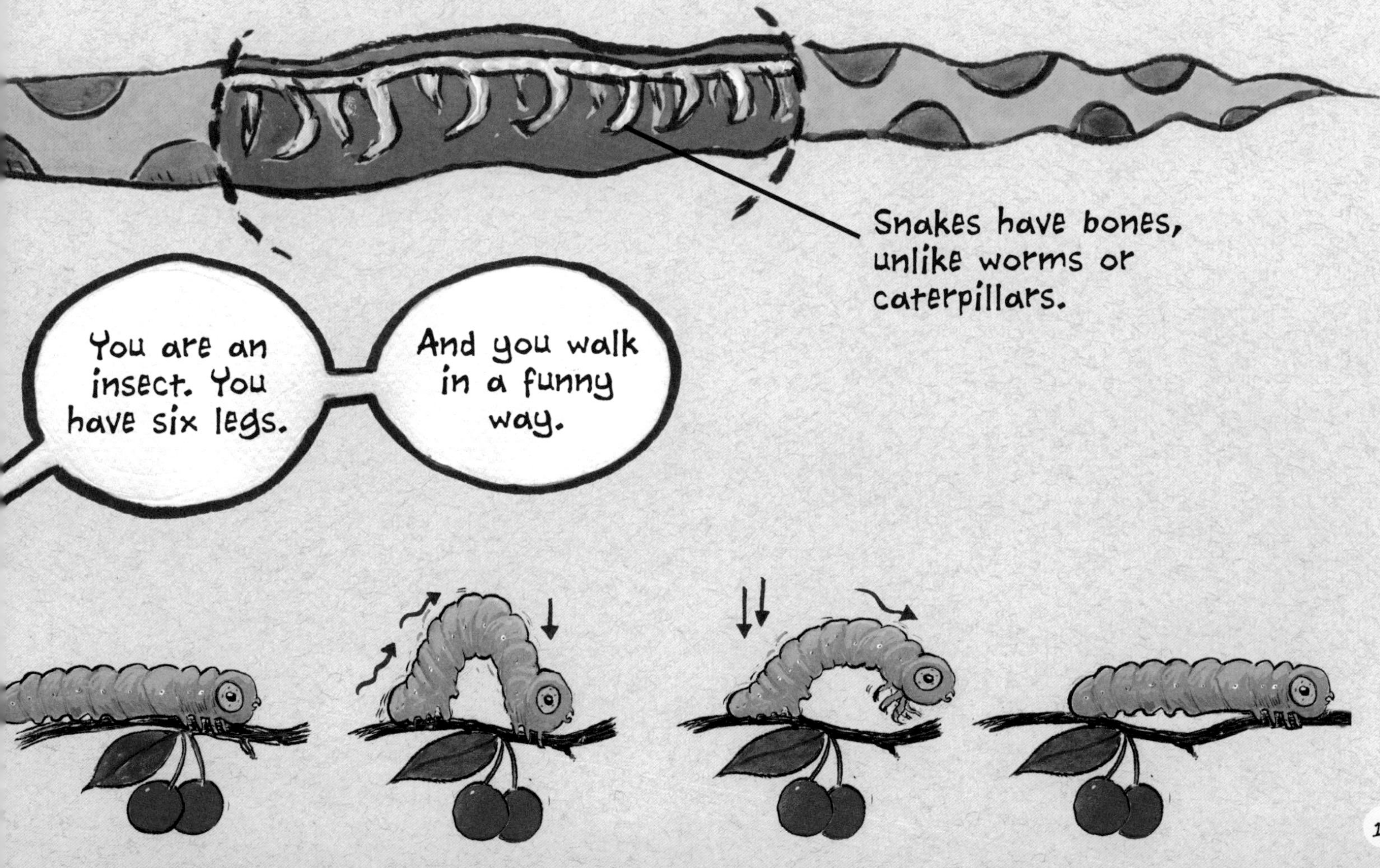
Snakes have bones, unlike worms or caterpillars.
You are an insect. You have six legs.
And you walk in a funny way.

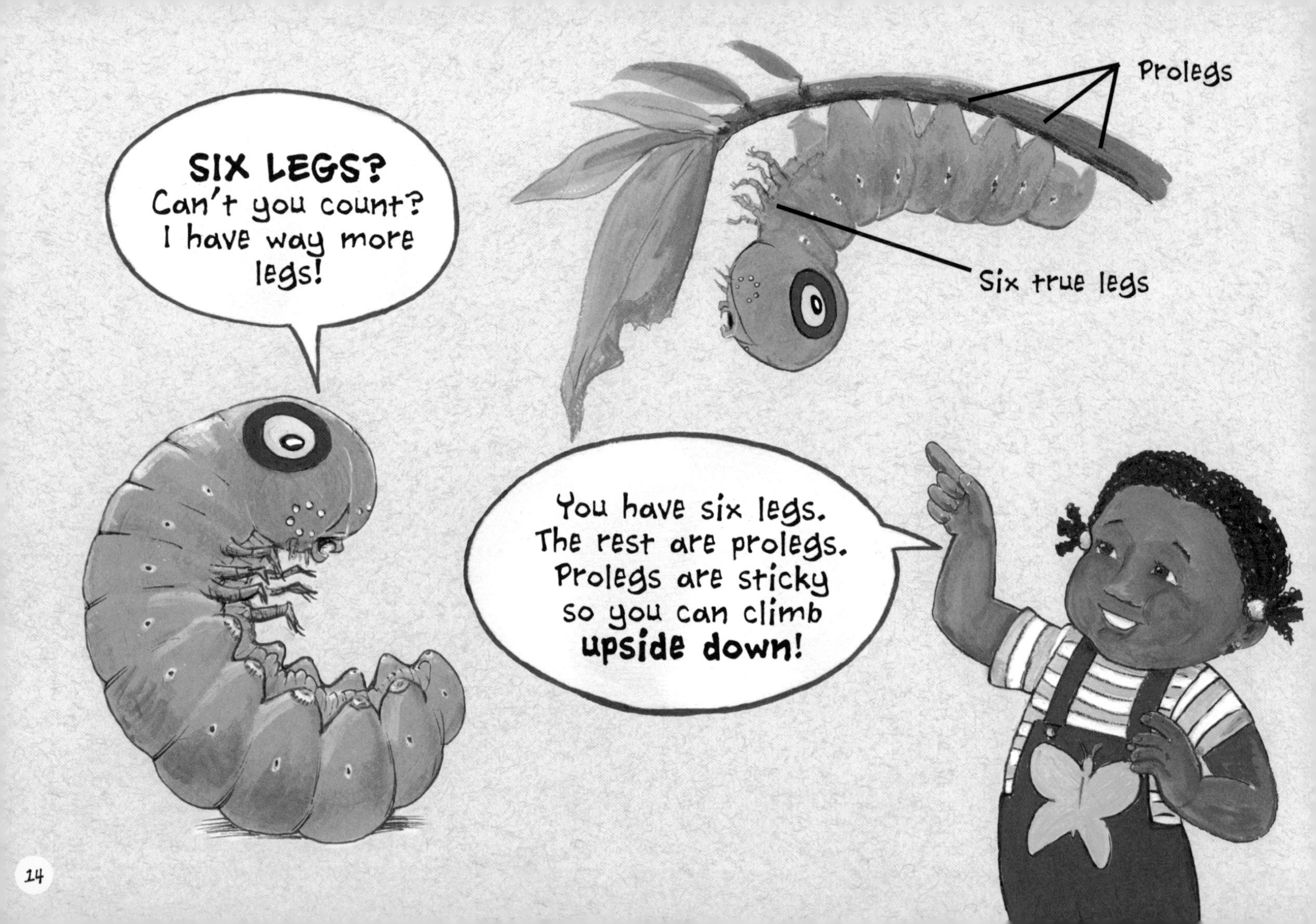

SIX LEGS? Can't you count? I have way more legs!
Prolegs
Six true legs
You have six legs. The rest are prolegs. Prolegs are sticky so you can climb **upside down!**

AND THEN,
ONE DAY,
THE ANSWER
COMES...

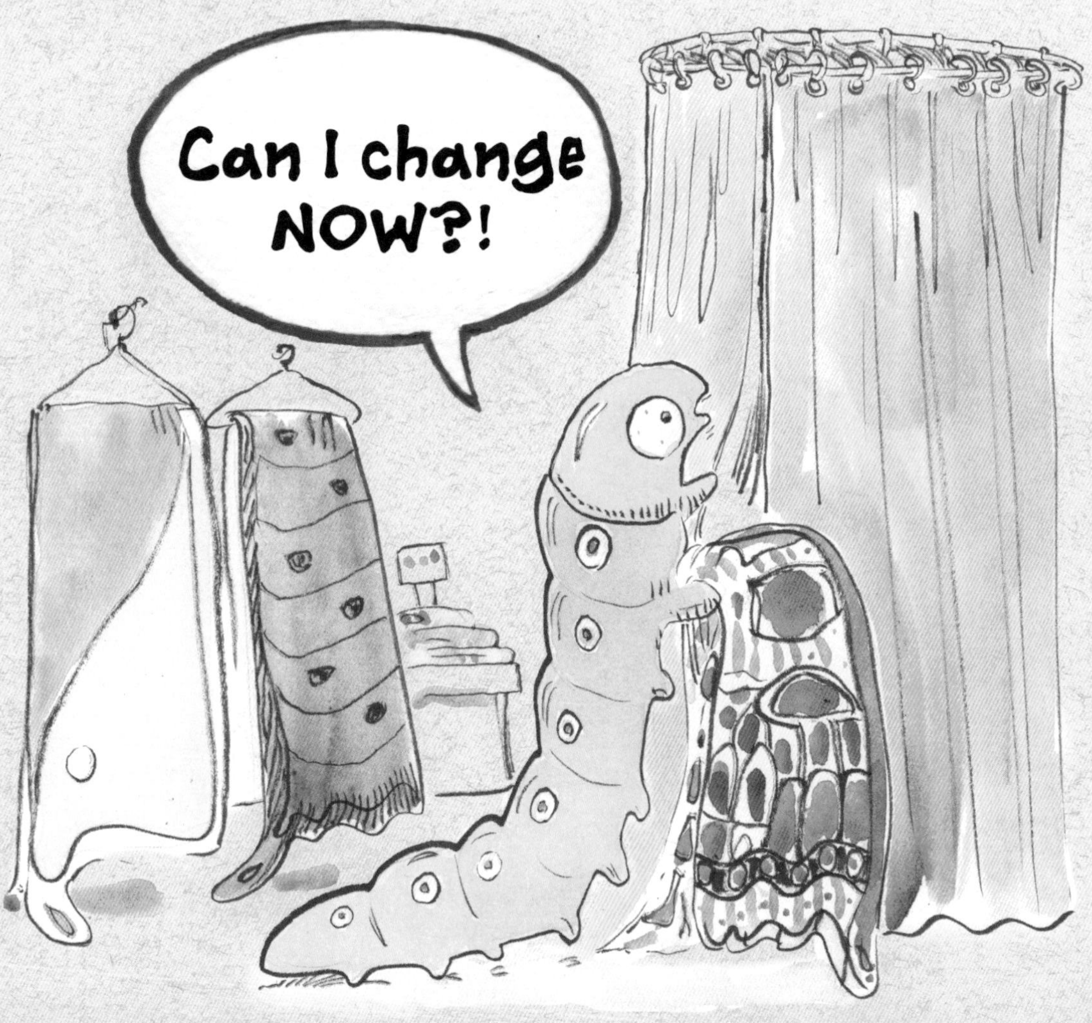
Can I change NOW?!

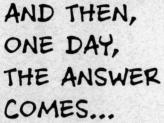

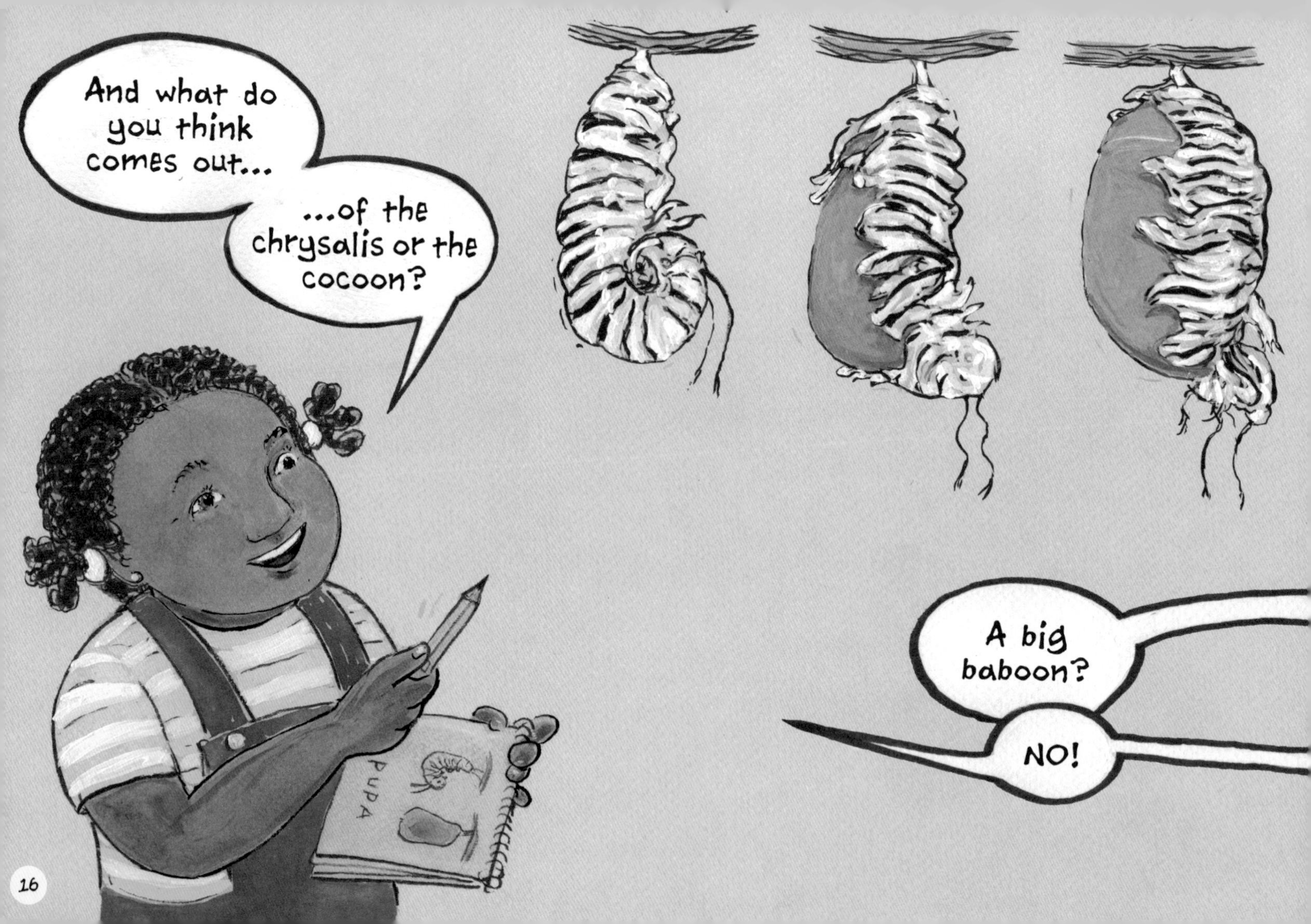
And what do you think comes out...
...of the chrysalis or the cocoon?
PUPA
A big baboon?
NO!

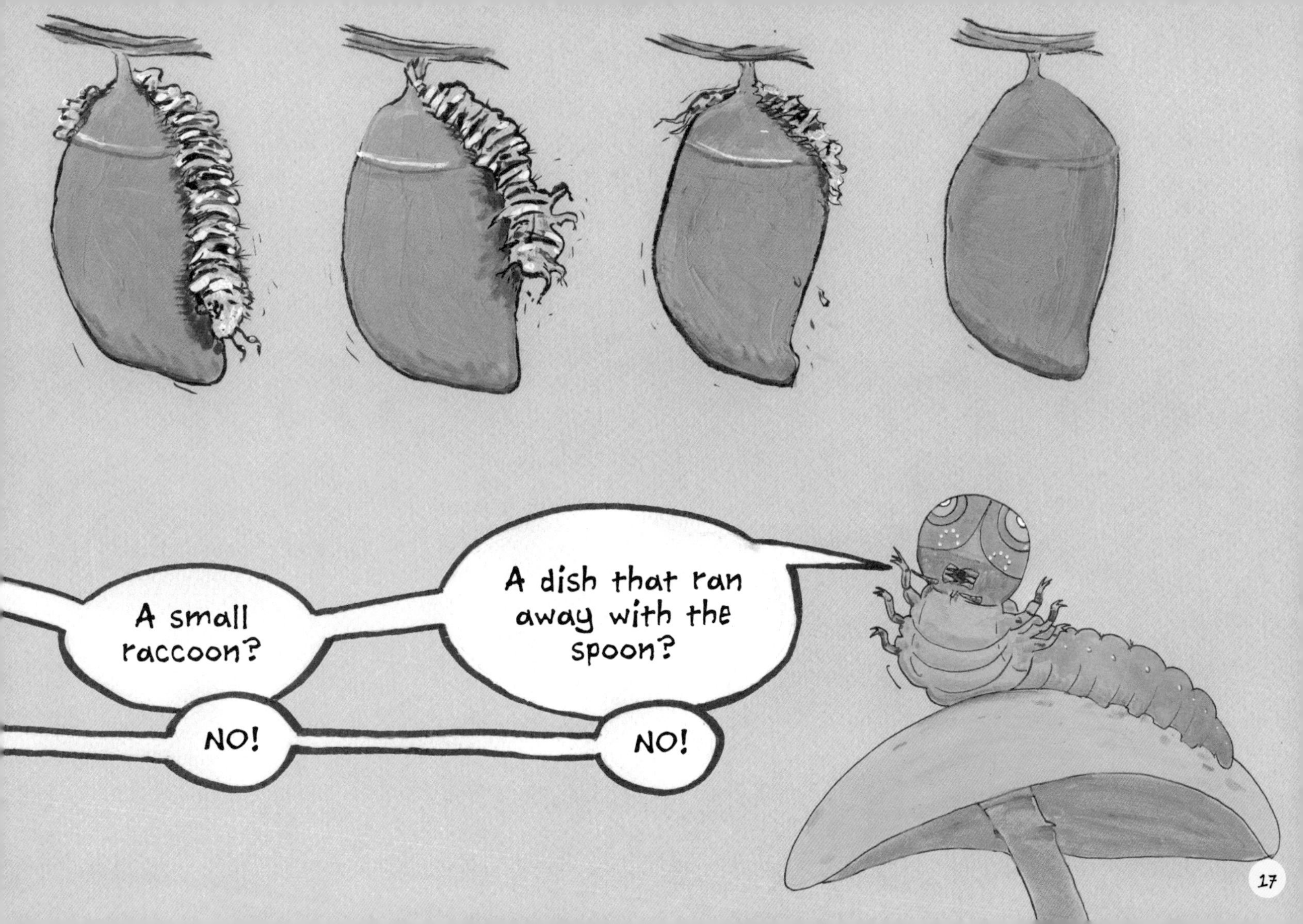
A small raccoon?
NO!
A dish that ran away with the spoon?
NO!

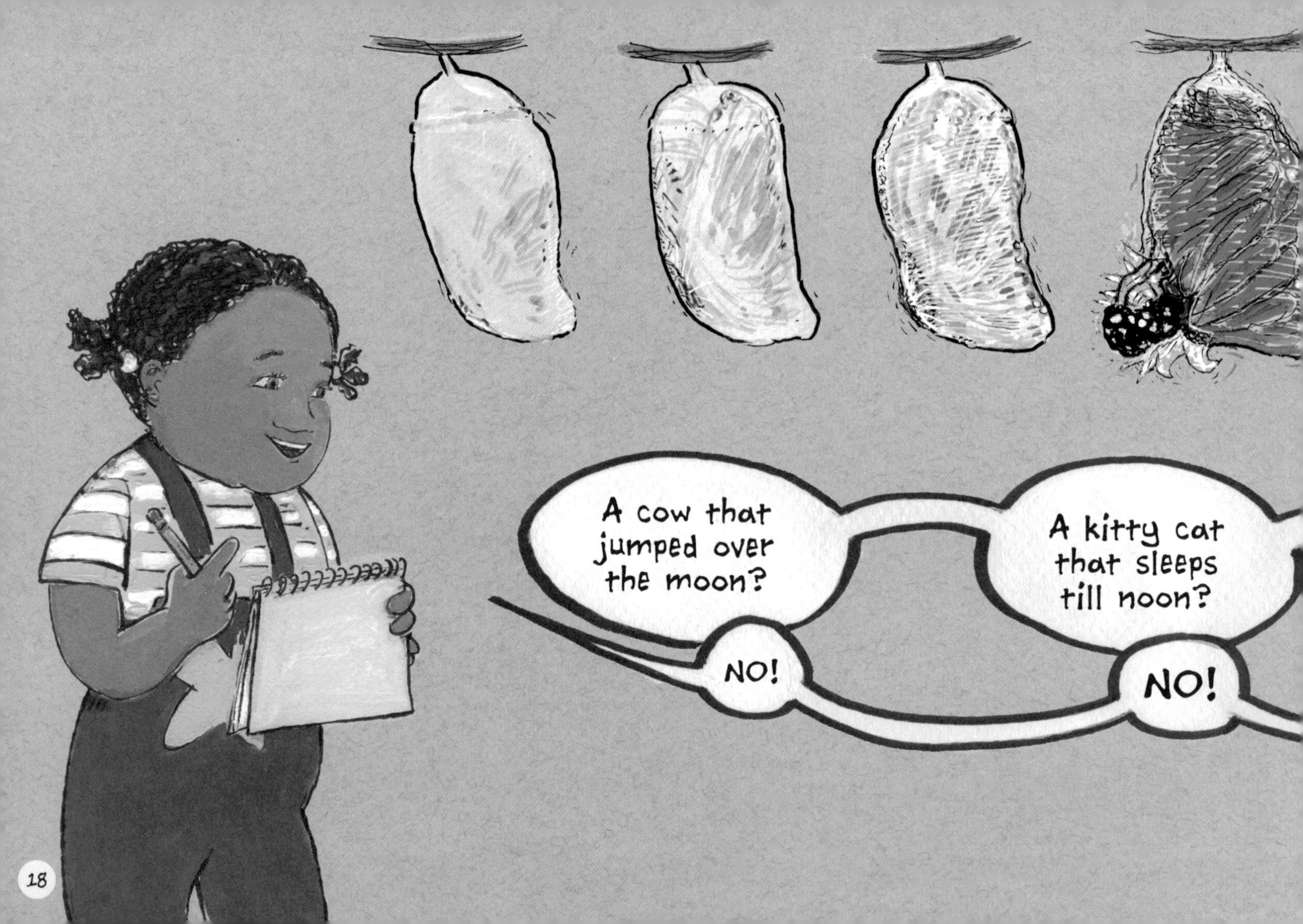

A cow that jumped over the moon?
A kitty cat that sleeps till noon?
NO!
NO!

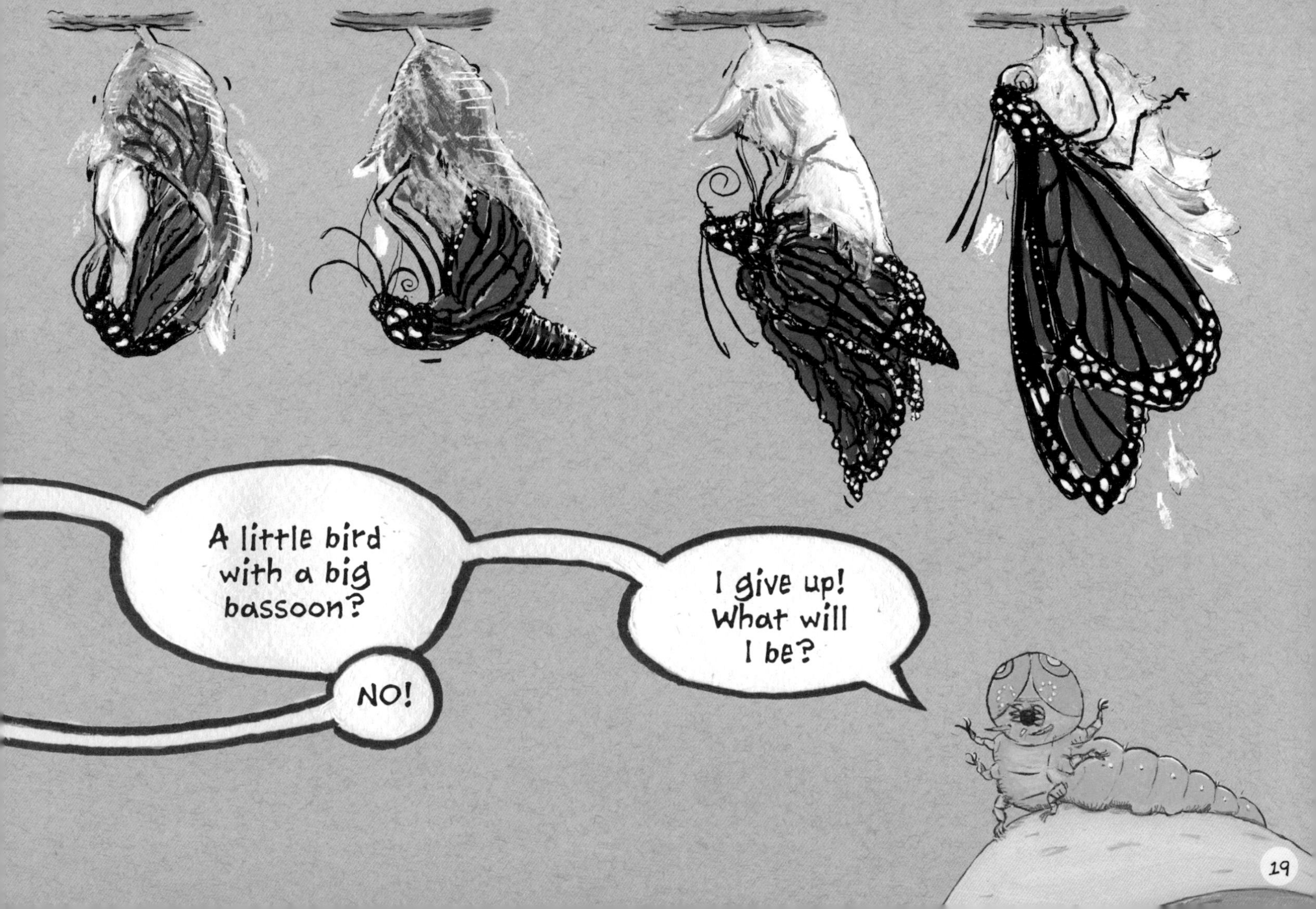
A little bird with a big bassoon?
NO!
I give up! What will I be?

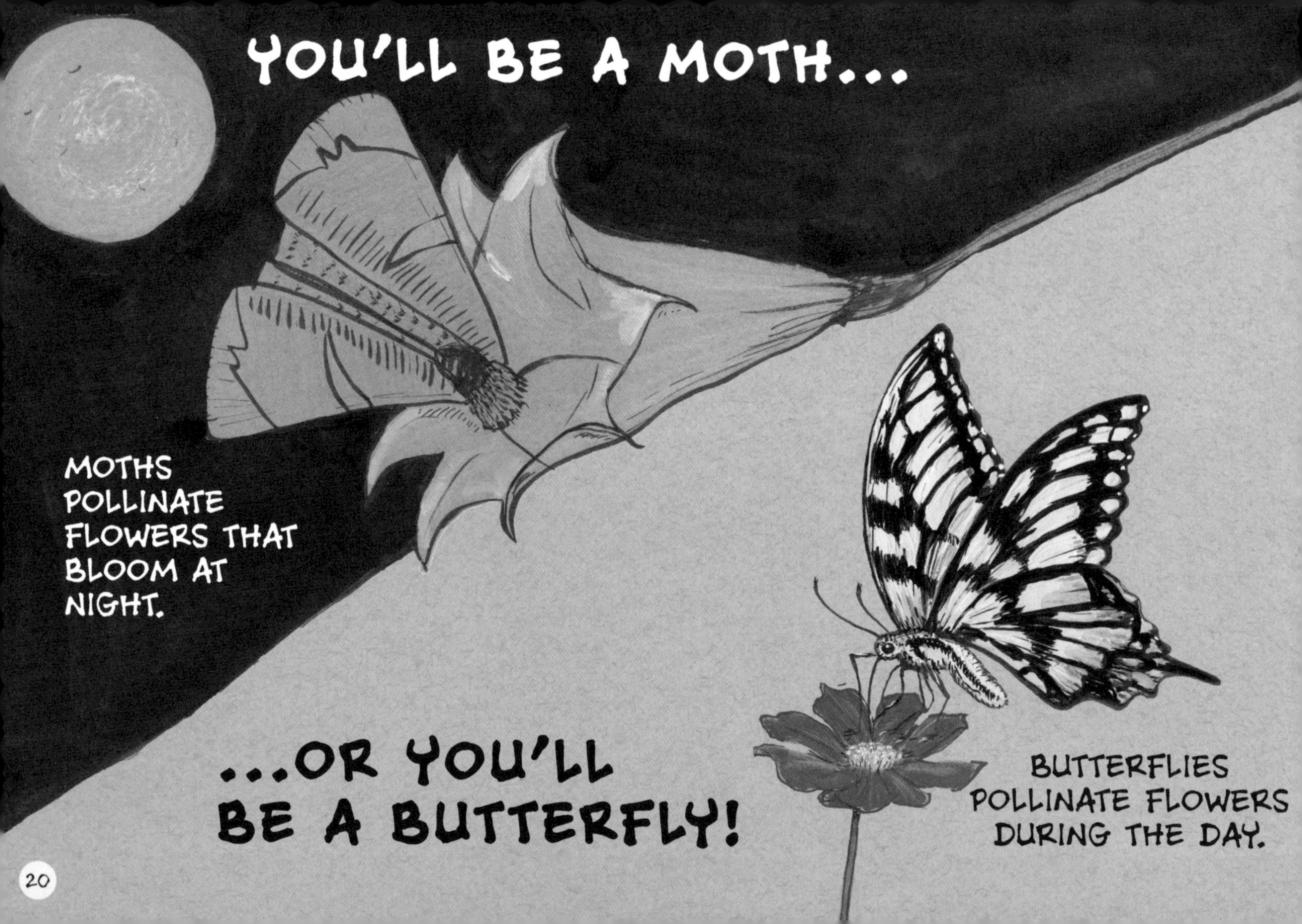

YOU'LL BE A MOTH...

MOTHS POLLINATE FLOWERS THAT BLOOM AT NIGHT.

...OR YOU'LL BE A BUTTERFLY!

BUTTERFLIES POLLINATE FLOWERS DURING THE DAY.

MOTHS AND BUTTERFLIES CAN LOOK A LOT ALIKE.

MOTHS REST WITH THEIR WINGS FLAT.

BUTTERFLIES REST WITH THEIR WINGS FOLDED.

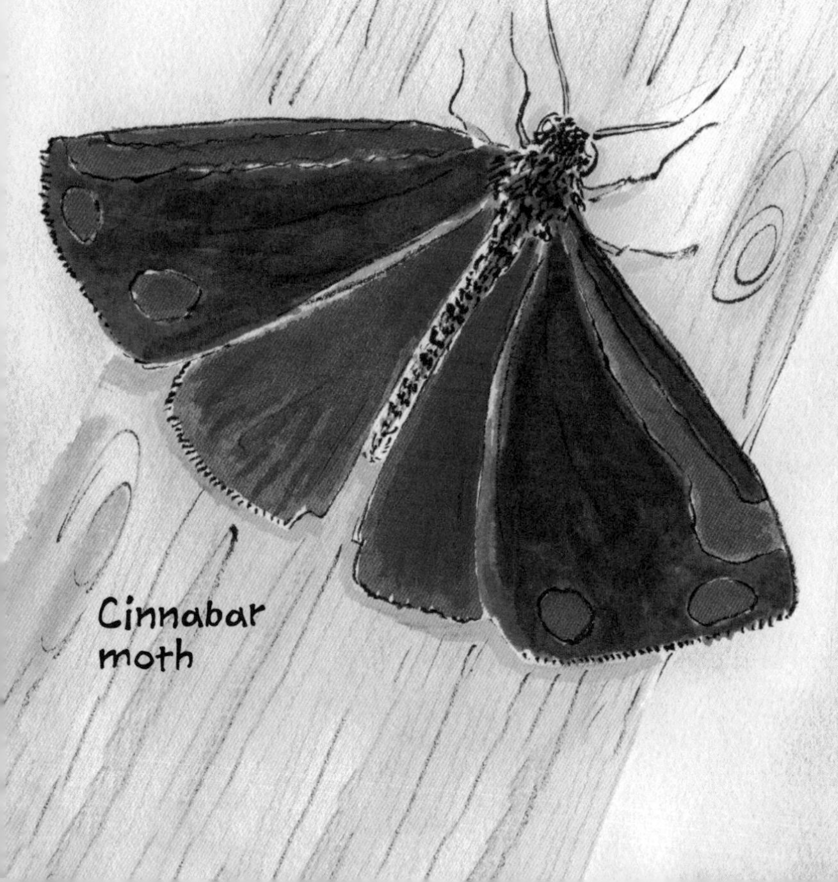

Cinnabar moth

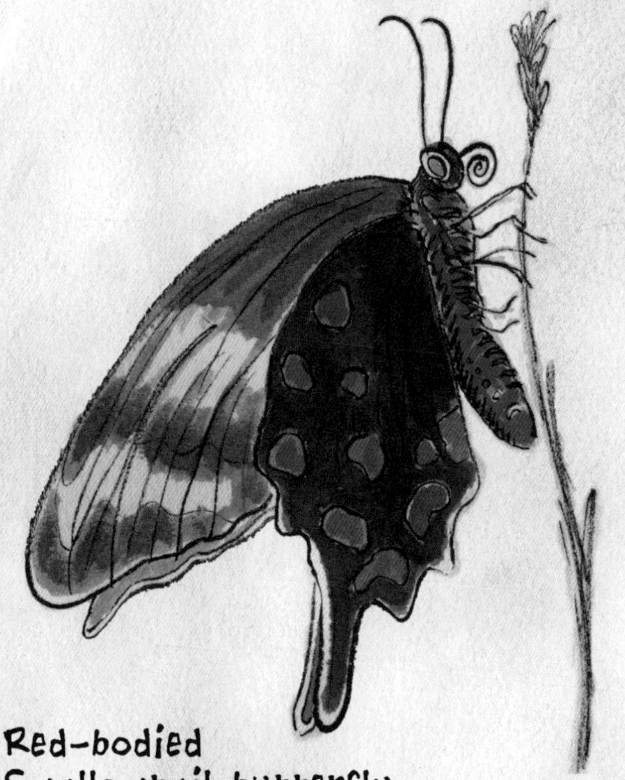

Red-bodied Swallowtail butterfly

MOTHS CAN BE BIG AND BEAUTIFUL.

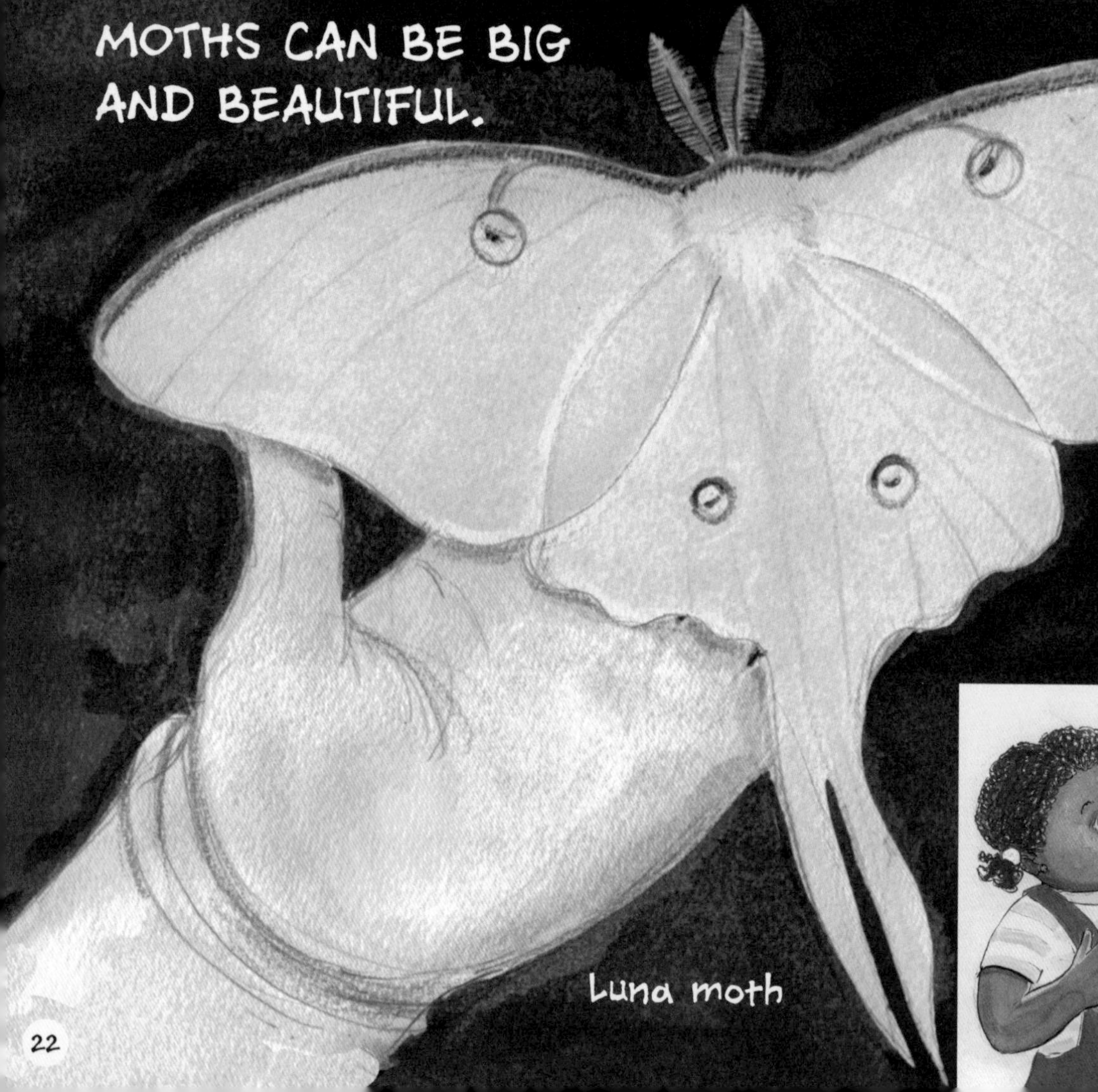
Luna moth

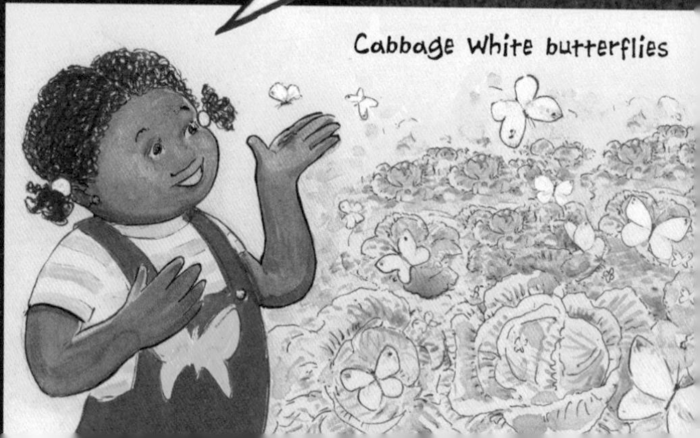
And butterflies can be tiny.
Cabbage White butterflies

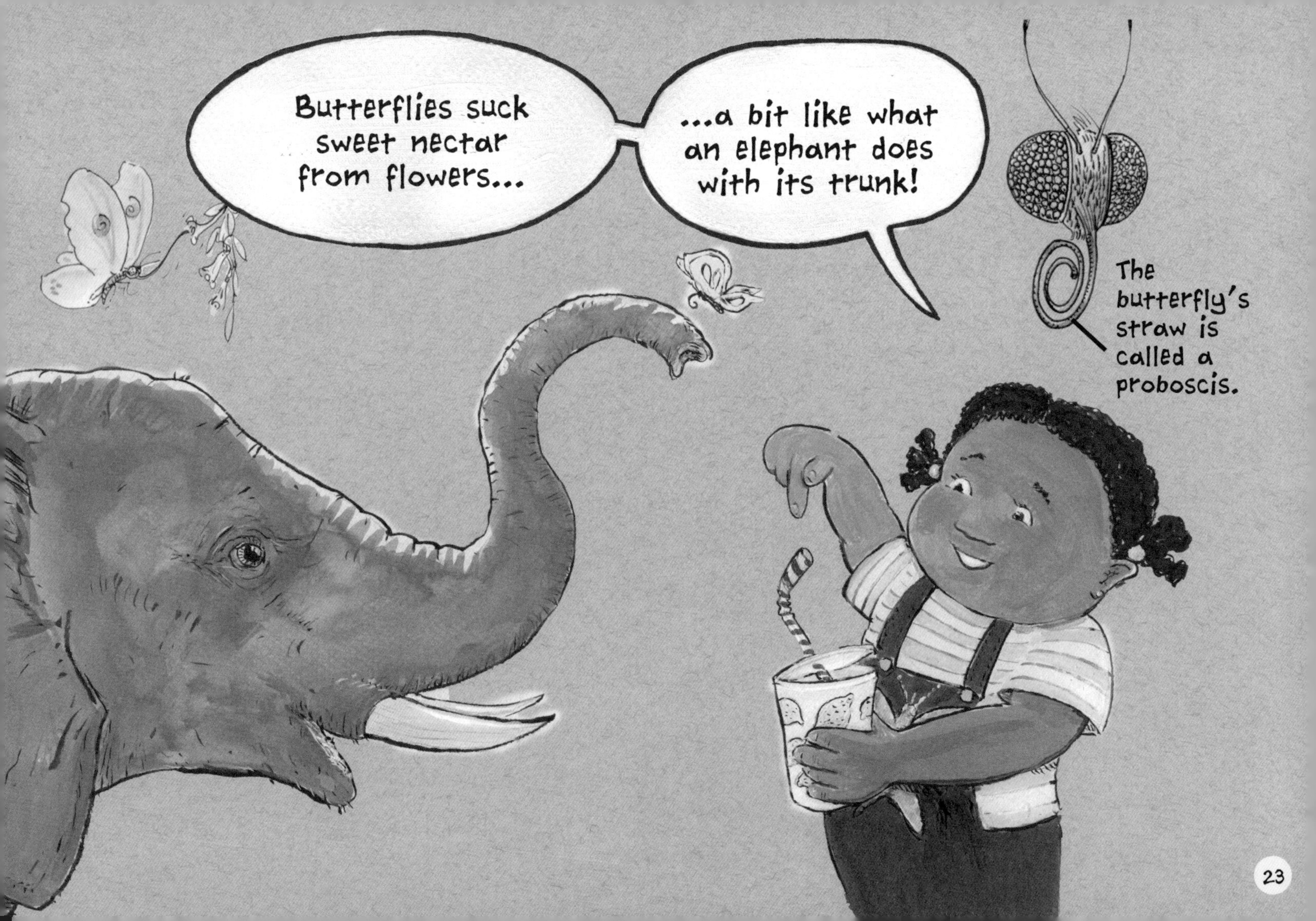
Butterflies suck sweet nectar from flowers...
...a bit like what an elephant does with its trunk!
The butterfly's straw is called a proboscis.

MAP OF A BUTTERFLY

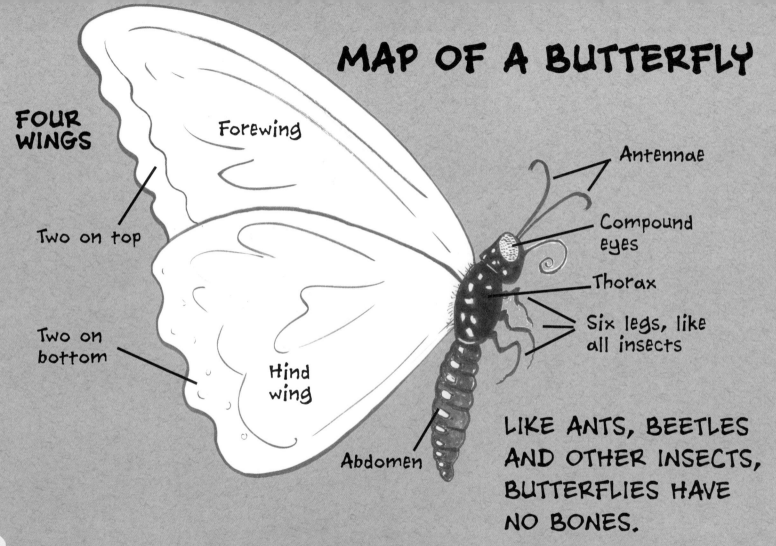

FOUR WINGS

Forewing

Two on top

Two on bottom

Hind wing

Abdomen

Antennae

Compound eyes

Thorax

Six legs, like all insects

LIKE ANTS, BEETLES AND OTHER INSECTS, BUTTERFLIES HAVE NO BONES.

Butterflies use their wings like ears to sense sounds.
And they smell and taste with their antennae and their feet!
YUM! YUM!

BUTTERFLY WINGS ARE CLEAR.

Their color comes from tiny scales covering the wings like roof tiles.

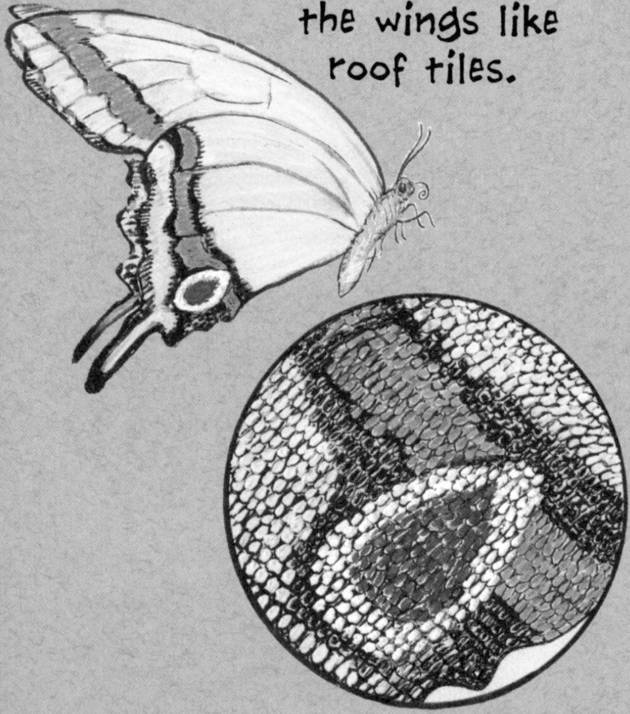

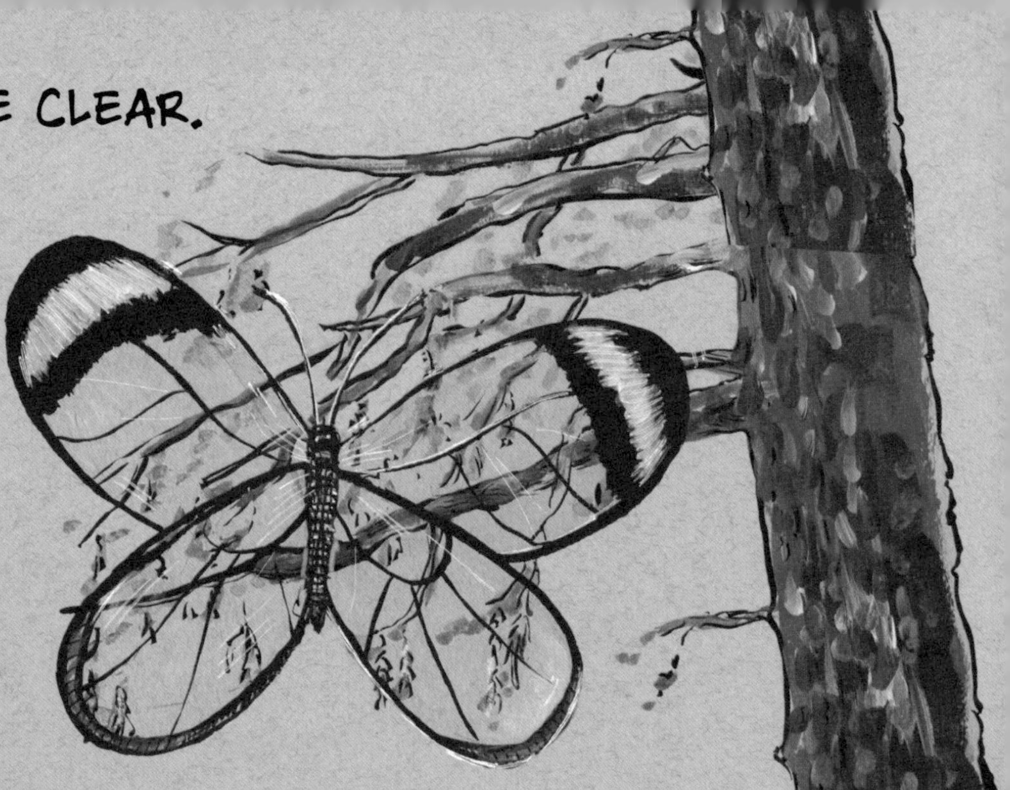

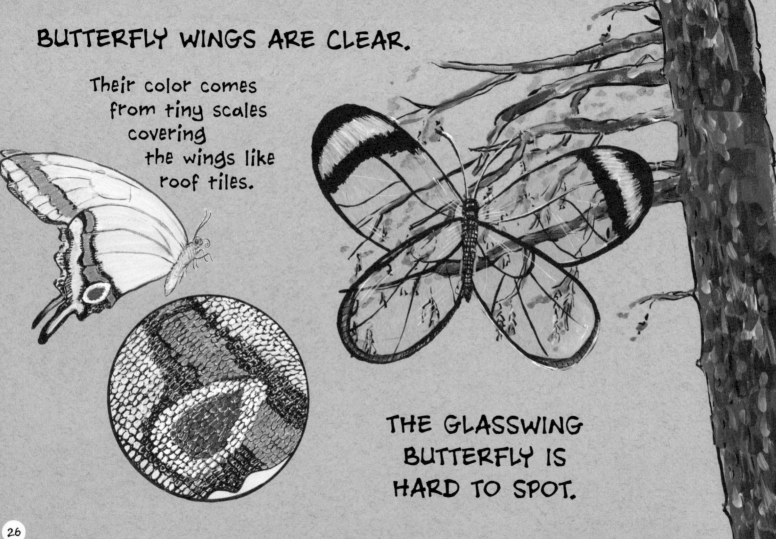

THE GLASSWING BUTTERFLY IS HARD TO SPOT.

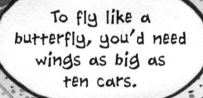

To fly like a butterfly, you'd need wings as big as ten cars.

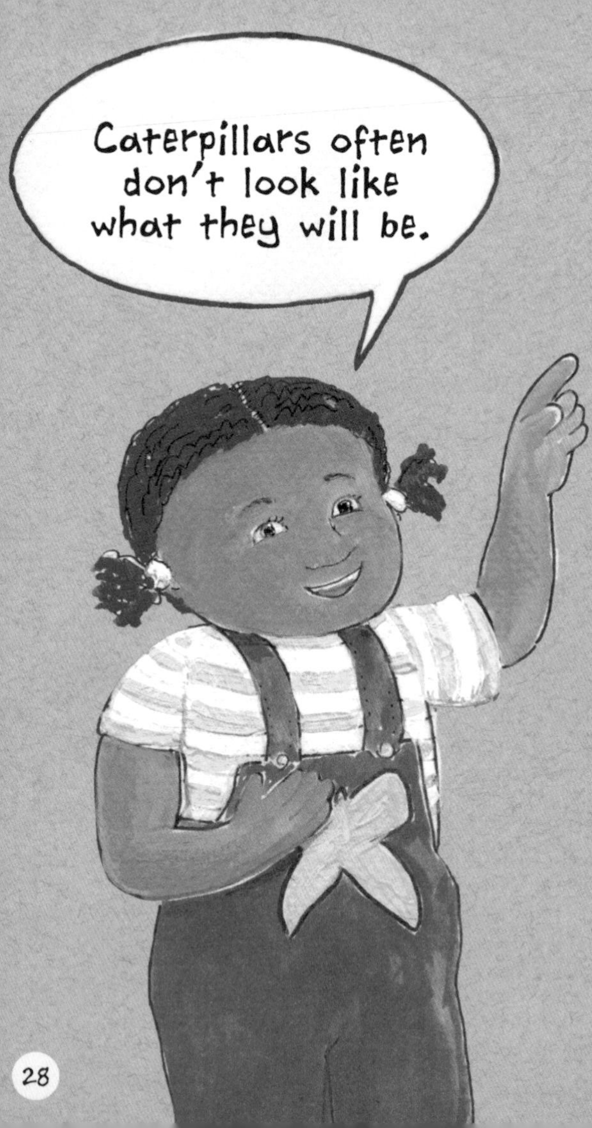
Caterpillars often don't look like what they will be.

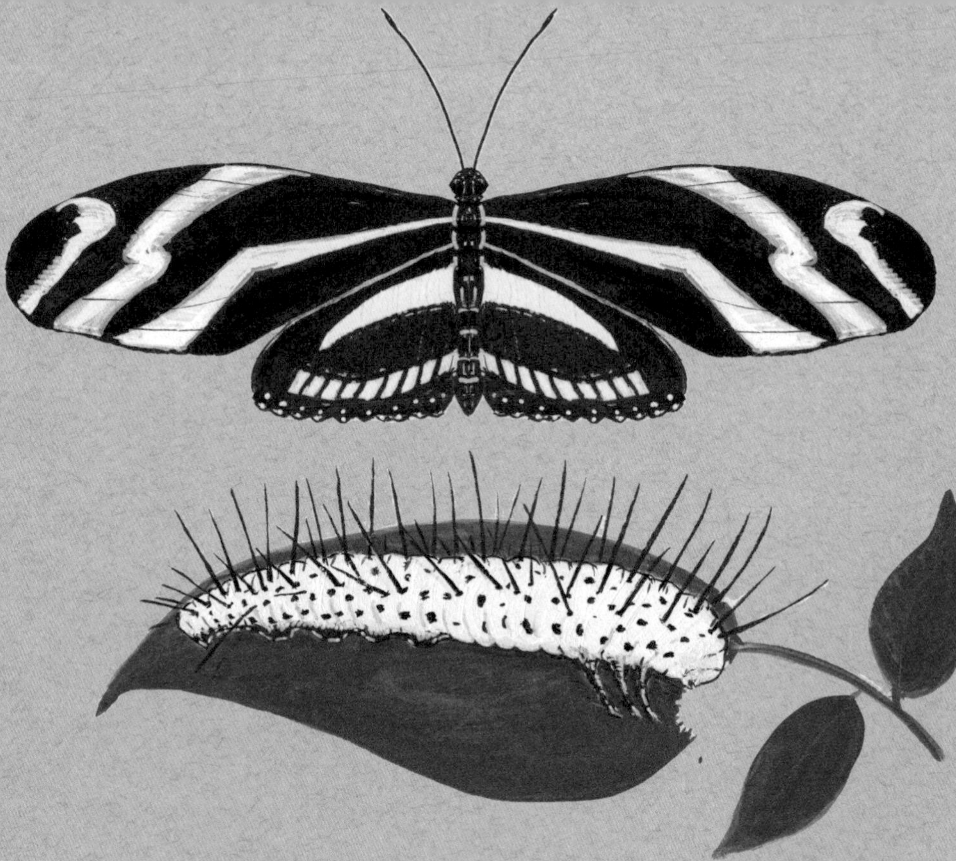

THE CATERPILLAR OF THE ZEBRA LONGWING BUTTERFLY IS ALL WHITE.

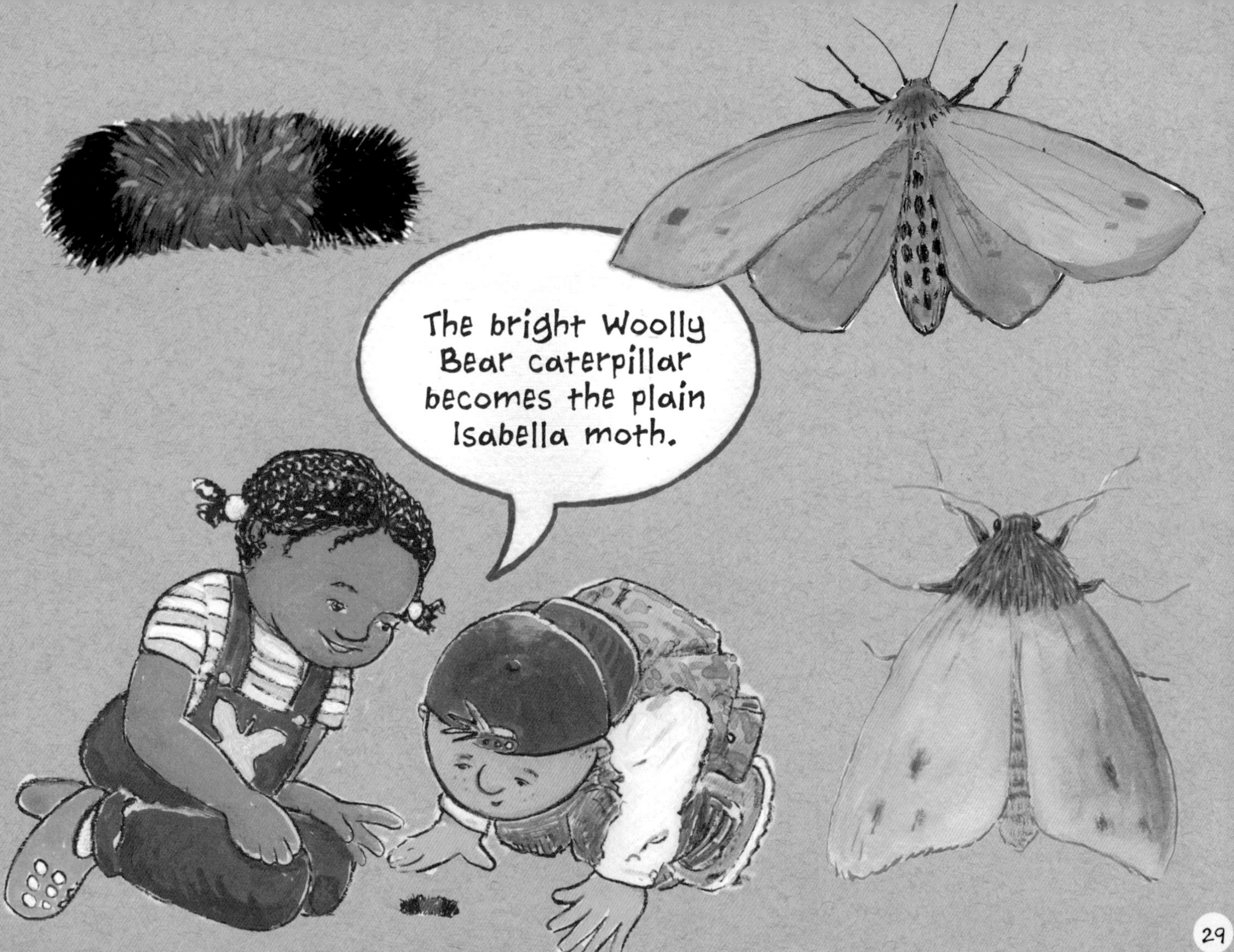
The bright Woolly Bear caterpillar becomes the plain Isabella moth.

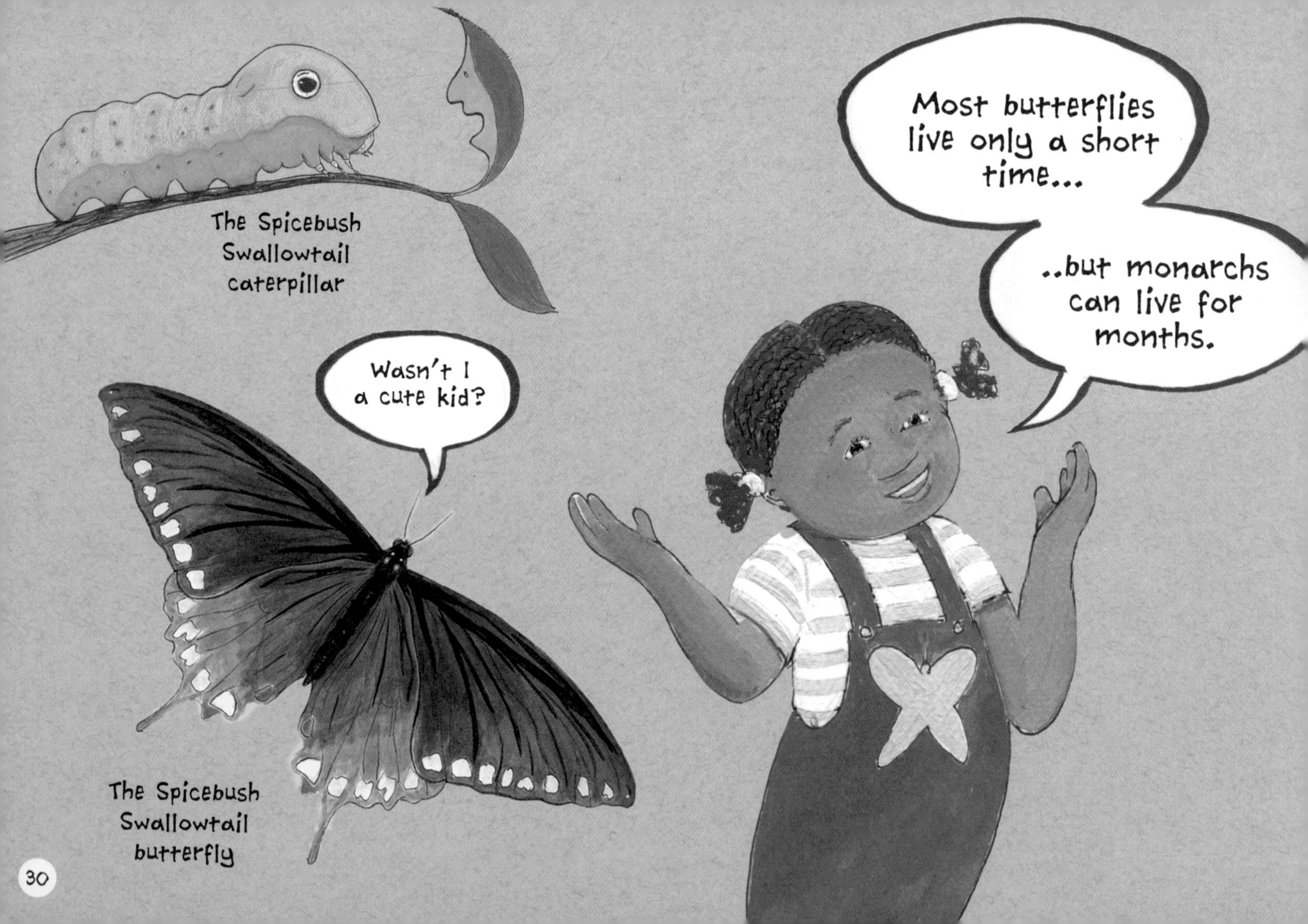
The Spicebush Swallowtail caterpillar
Most butterflies live only a short time...
..but monarchs can live for months.
Wasn't I a cute kid?
The Spicebush Swallowtail butterfly

SOME MONARCHS MIGRATE FOR THOUSANDS OF MILES.

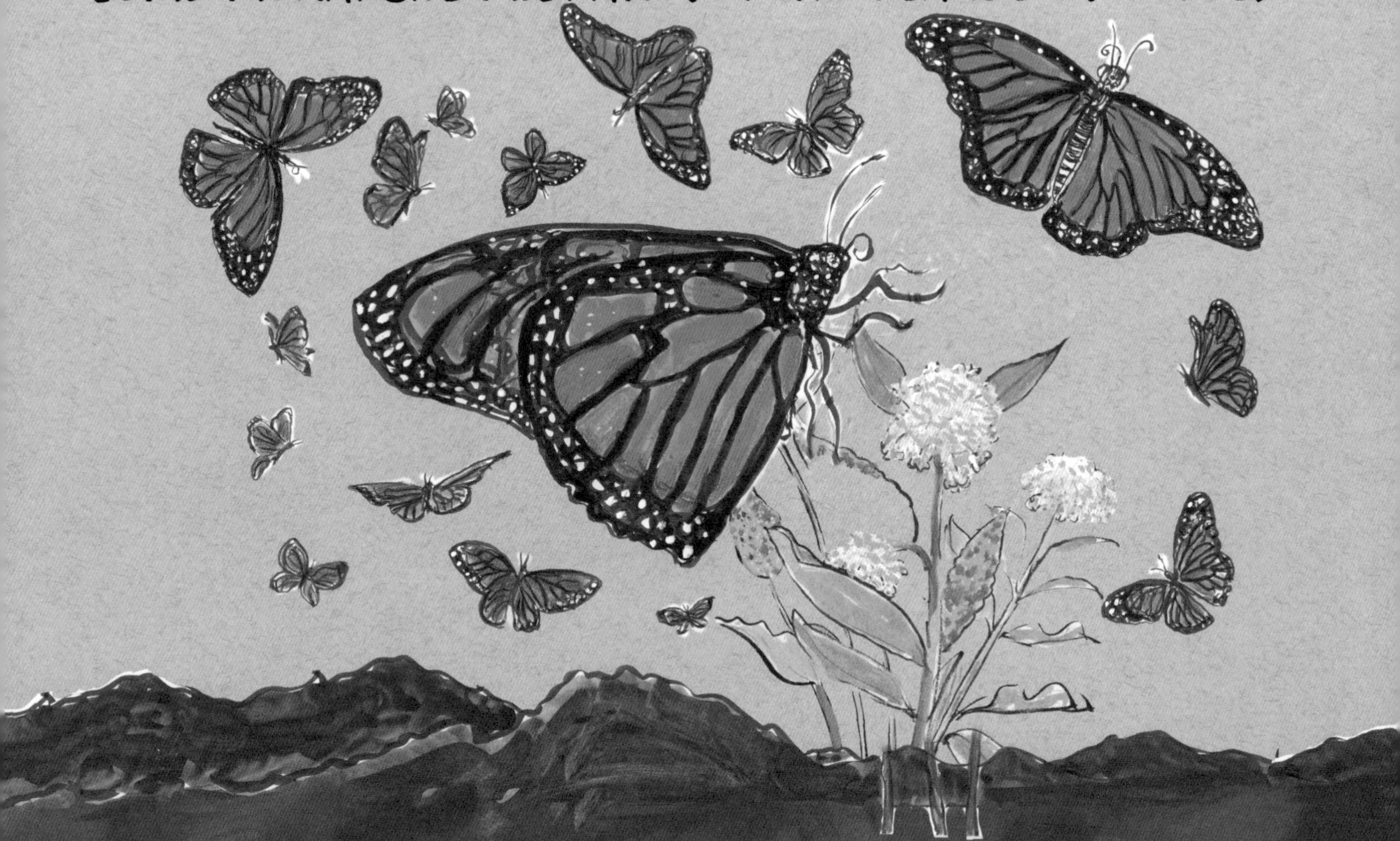

FROM THE USA OR CANADA, THEY FLY TO MEXICO FOR THE WINTER.

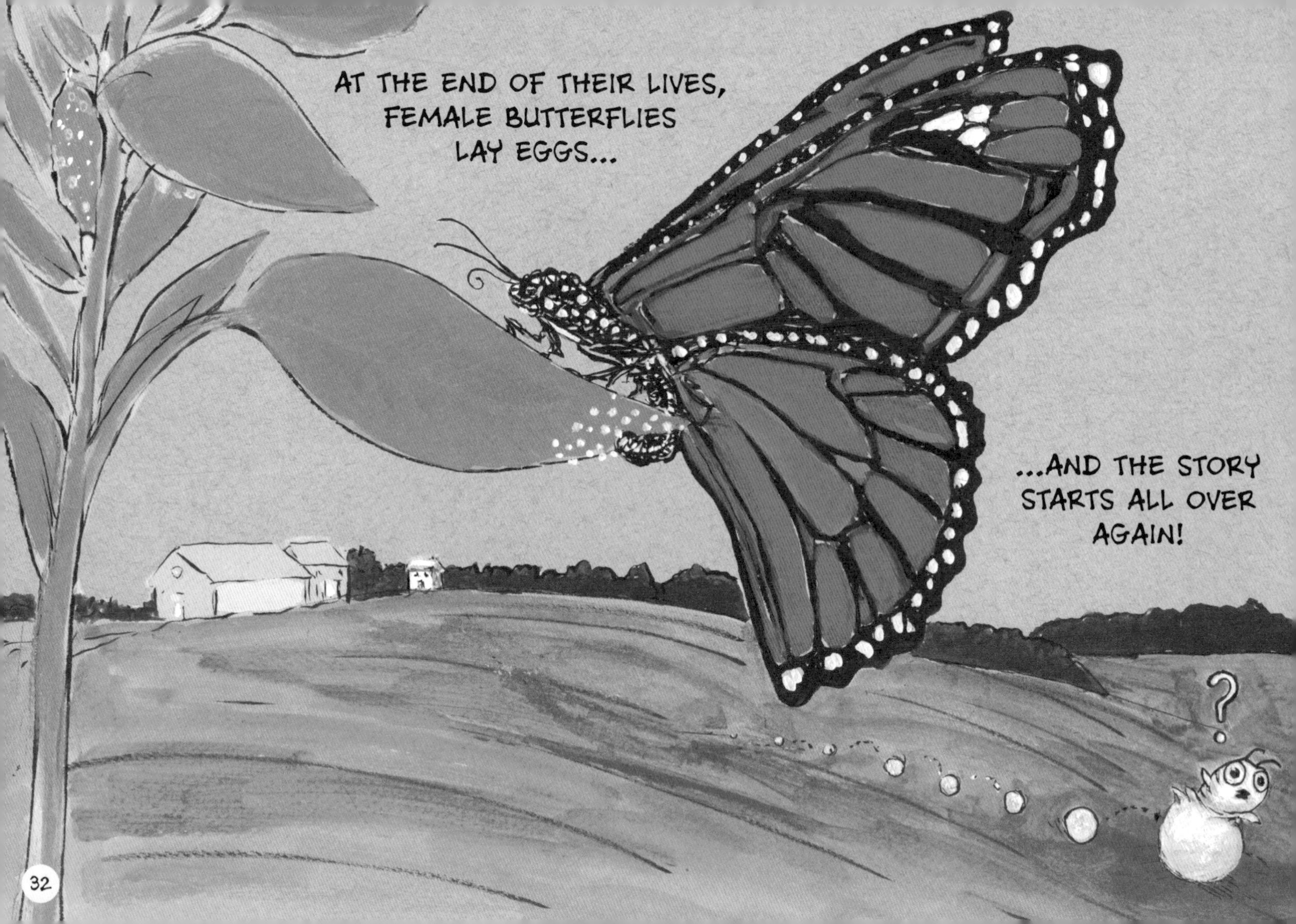
AT THE END OF THEIR LIVES, FEMALE BUTTERFLIES LAY EGGS...
...AND THE STORY STARTS ALL OVER AGAIN!
?